MW00965763

Contents

This is my own personal faith journey that I have traveled thus far. God-willing, the journey will continue, and as I grow in faith, I am learning how to read the signs of direction that God gives to us all. In life, there are no such things as a coincident they are assuredly God winks.

First, a little background on me. I was born and raised in the city of Detroit. My parents were Mary (Nader) and Pat Everhart (I was named after both of them Patricia Mary).

I had a large family; my parents had six children, I am the second youngest.

We had a hardworking dad who earned a decent living and a mom that stayed at home. We all went to church together—sounds perfect, right? In spite of the fact my dad was a drinker, I feel I had an overall good Christian example from my parents.

Real Life Begins

I met my first husband in high school. He liked to drink and carry on, but it was the seventies; everyone did, me included. After two years of marriage, Brad was born, and when he was only six months old, I became pregnant again with my daughter Stacy. I was physically the best mom I could be, as they were always clean, fed, and when we went out, we were always prepared for anything. My then-husband and I would still do the partying thing and entertaining at our home as well. It was when the children got to be about two and three that I started going back to church. I started to change over the next couple years, and we moved to an area closer to my siblings. When my children started catechism, I volunteered, and although I was teaching others, it was I who was the true student and began a deepening of my faith that still to this day continues. God was preparing and strengthening me for what laid ahead.

My husband's alcoholism continued to escalate, and as it turns out, God had put me in the right neighborhood and at the right church. My neighbor whose husband was a recovering alcoholic invited the kids and me to go to an Al-Anon and Alatot meeting. That meeting changed my life. I thought I was going to help the alcoholic and found I could only help myself, and I needed *quite a bit of work*. I always say that out of my siblings, I was the only one blessed to have married an alcoholic. I was able to understand that it is a sickness, which improved my relationship with my own father dramatically. I then understood him in a new light. I also learned that my dad had given me something that most of the adult children of alcoholics never got! Some way, somehow, he got it across to me that he loved me, and beyond a doubt, I knew it.

The alcoholic I was married to was getting progressively worse. He seemed to almost lead two separate lives. He would attend church with us and even played his congas in the church folk group. But things started to get scary.

He would miss work, lose jobs, go missing for hours or sometimes days. He went in and out of treatment centers and then relapsed. I knew things were getting bad, and I had no skill or career. My first real example of God having a hand in my life was soon to begin.

A friend of mine talked me into taking a real estate class and getting my license so I could time-share a job with her for a builder. I took the money out of my children's savings account, took the course, and passed it. I passed the test the first time I took it and got my license. The builder, however, wanted me to do things that I felt were morally questionable, and I literally thought to myself, *I do not think when I die God will ask how much money I have in the bank or what kind of house I owned.* I quit after working only two weeks and felt I had wasted my children's money on the real estate course. This story will continue later.

For the next couple years, I continued to be active at church, teaching and taking communion to people in the hospital. At the same time, I joined a group called the Legion of Mary and visited the lonely, both homebound and individuals in nursing homes. I met a lot of great people, and some I even discovered strange connections with. For example, a lonely gentleman in a nursing home, with no living family members had lived on the same street I grew up on, and ushered at the Catholic Church where I went to grade school. Some say with God there are no coincidences, and I believe that. During this time of my life, my first tragedy was about to unfold.

My younger brother had his second child, Ian, and I was chosen to be his godmother. Ian always had a problem with his bowel movements, and after my sister-in-law persisted for six months, the doctors diagnosed him with a disorder called Hirschsprung's Disease. A colostomy was scheduled, with the plan being to reverse it later. A week prior to his scheduled surgery, my brother Larry and his wife

Mary Ann took him to the emergency room. He was sick with flu-type symptoms, and because of his background, his parents were concerned. They released him on paper, but Mary Ann did not feel he looked right and wanted to feed him (she was breastfeeding at the time). Ian went into convulsions, and they flew him by helicopter to Mott Children's Hospital in Ann Arbor. The feces had backed up into his body and caused brain damage. It was a long process to get him back home, and he had feeding tubes, an ileostomy bag, and was what some would refer to as a vegetable.

Evelyn's Story

My next real tragedy came when my sister Evelyn, a mother of six, got sick. The doctors were puzzled, and she was in a lot of pain but still forcing herself to go to work, take night classes, and take care of her husband and son. She finally went to the emergency room when her leg swelled up and hardened. They opened her up, and she was so filled with cancer they did nothing and closed her back up. That was a Friday afternoon, and she died that Sunday at one in the morning. She talked to all six of her children and said good-bye and then asked to be taken off the blood thinners. As Pope John Paul said, he had his bags packed when he knew he was dying. Evelyn surely had her bags packed and was right with God. This was my first real lesson from God: We should *always* have our bags packed.

Knowing her cheerful and loving spirit, this did not surprise me. She had a deep faith and all who knew her could see it through her words and actions. Her children said after she passed away, they all went with their dad back home. The time was around 3:00 AM, and they saw a white dove fly to their driveway. It stayed there for hours! It is unusual for this to take place at night, and especially odd since the house was on a main road and there was lots of traffic. This dove, despite the traffic, didn't move for hours. This was Sunday, May 1, 1988.

The wake and funeral were hard. My then-husband Larry was drinking most of the time he was there, and my family began to realize things were not quite as they should be.

My Dad's Story

My father had been in the same hospital as Evelyn and had been fighting congestive heart failure due to damage from his own alcoholism. In 1987, they had told him he had about six months to live, but he died two years later. It was hard on my parents to lose Evelyn, and I heard my dad even ask God why it couldn't have been him. Well, God's answer to that came later. I think God knew Mom needed him to get through Evelyn's death, but even more important, God was giving him time to think and pray.

The nun from Mom and Dad's church would come on Saturday's and bring communion to Dad. One Saturday, the sister brought the newly ordained priest along with her, and Dad asked if he could talk with him and give his confession. The young priest agreed. Dad had a stroke the next day, went into a coma for a couple days, and then passed away while my Mom, my brother Joe, and his wife Judy were holding his hands and praying the Our Father. He died June 1, 1989. The young priest really felt that this was God at work and even spoke of it that way during the funeral mass—the young priest's very first funeral mass. God was wonderful to give my dad that gift of forgiveness and grace.

Ian's Story

When baby Ian had gotten sick, I had shared his story with my friends in the Legion of Mary and they prayed with me. One day, a friend from the group gave me a book called *The Power of the Powerless* and said that she had gotten it in the mail, although she never ordered it. She felt God intended it for me. I read this book in one night.

A short synopsis of the book is the author, Chris DeVink, had a brother who was much like Ian (what they referred to back then as a vegetative state). He was engaged to be married and needed to tell his fiancé that it would be his responsibility to take care of his brother if anything happened to his parents. She, upon finding this out, broke off the engagement. Later, the author had met someone and was starting to get serious about her. He invited her for dinner with his family and then took her upstairs to meet his brother. He explained the situation of him being responsible when his parents passed away. Instead of being turned off by it, she literally took the spoon and bowl and said, "Here, let me feed him."

That is what the author called "the power of the powerless". We call this person a vegetable, and yet he could see right through to the soul of the two women and help his brother pick the good-hearted woman for his wife! At this point in time, my brother Larry felt God might be punishing him with Ian's situation. But after he read the book, he felt there was a purpose and could see all the good things that came from it.

Baby Ian had been predicated to have a lifespan of eighteen years, but the night after my brother read the book, and only two nights after I read it, Ian got pneumonia, was hospitalized, and passed away March 11, 1990. Larry and Mary Ann read through the book and loved it. The next day, Ian who was three years old, died from pneumonia. But not until my brother got the message God was trying to give him. God will use us in his plan if we are open to it.

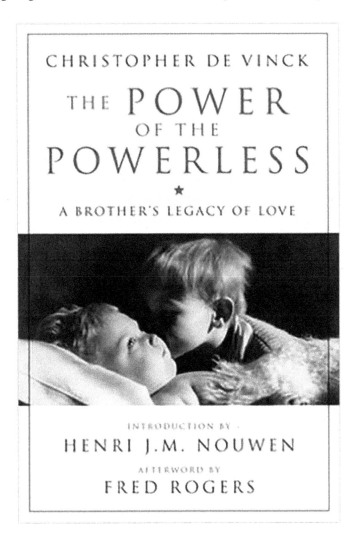

My sister Anita and I were asked to plan the funeral and found the priest to be very cold. He reluctantly agreed to let me speak about Ian at the end of the funeral mass. I literally wrote what I wanted to say in less than fifteen minutes. I felt that it was the Holy Spirit that wrote this, and I was just the vehicle. I am including a copy of it below:

Ian's Eulogy

On September 1, 1986, a beautiful baby boy was born. But at that time we had no idea of the way Ian would draw love, courage, compassion, and understanding from those who were close to him.

Then, one sad day in March of 1987, when he was only six months old, things changed. During a two-month hospital stay and four surgeries later, Baby Ian was not the same. Some things did not change and even increased—and that was the attentiveness and love he received from his parents.

Mary Ann and Larry did everything possible to help Ian progress, but they soon learned that with the seizures being uncontrolled, he could not retain what he was learning. Most would have given up, but not Ian's parents. They were constant in trying to show him love and make him smile or laugh. It wasn't often he smiled, but the feeling he gave you when he did was always worth the patient wait. Always concerned about his physical condition, Mary Ann would cart Ian all the way across town to Barnum, one of the best schools in Michigan. No, it wasn't easy, but Mary Ann did it anyway. THAT IS LOVE.

Ian and his routine became such a part of their lives that Justin even learned to help care for him and was so used to loving Ian that when Mary Ann would bring him to Justin's school, he wouldn't think twice about telling his friends about Ian in his matter-of-fact way. Justin simply loved Ian.

Ian was soon to have a new brother, Douglas, who, at only eighteen months, would help Mom or Dad with Ian by fetching diapers. Douglas simply loved Ian.

There were many others who were touched by this child who loved to be held and talked to. Ian gave back to us too, as he helped us to realize the true order of priorities in life. Maybe he even helped inspire some of us to be more patient. And I know he certainly touched his Aunt Patty's heart and has helped make her the loving and compassionate pediatrician she is now. Someone so powerless like Ian brought out such beautiful things from everyone he touched. Beyond a doubt, that was why he was with us. In three and a half years, he taught many of us more about life than we could learn in a lifetime.

by Patricia M. Sherrill

As at all children's funerals, the church was packed. I was a little nervous when I went up to speak; it almost felt surreal. I literally saw Evelyn, my dad, and Ian and they went up to the pulpit with me. They were all dressed in "dazzling" white and Ian was very healthy, standing straight up and alert. I felt filled with the Holy Spirit and the words just rattled off; they moved many people, including the cold priest who was openly weeping. That was truly the Holy Spirit sent from God our Father who authored the eulogy.

This is a song "Angel Face" that I wrote for Ian shortly after his death. The lyrics precede the actual music. Larry and Mary Ann put Ian's picture on his tombstone with the words "Angel Face" below it based on this song.

Refrain:

Angel face full of grace such an angel to me
Angel face full of grace now a real angel he'll be.

Verse I

Baby Ian with a future so bright we had no way of knowing his fight.
He was only six months and the world fell apart and baby Ian had to
make a new start

Verse II

He would never talk and he would never walk. But love he'd never be
without
He taught us things that we never knew. I guess that's what it's all about

Verse III

Ian lives with God now he was only three
Ian feels no more pain now he is truly free.
Here on earth we miss him and sometimes we cry
But he brought us such love that we never ask God why.

My Real Estate Career and Divorce

The alcoholic I was married to continued to get worse. I felt at the time I got my real estate license that it was a complete waste of my children's money, but little did I know that this would save my life when I needed it. I may have not known, but of course, God knew. Try to remember this story and not put judgment on things happening in your life, this is a prime example of thinking something is a bad thing and then finding out later it was truly a great thing.

I was attending Al-Anon meetings and getting stronger emotionally and spiritually. I was still singing in the church choir, teaching catechism, and working part-time in group homes as a caretaker. I remember feeling like such a good Catholic that I did not think I could ever divorce. It was not until I was on a religious retreat that the priest said it was not God's intention for me to smash my head against a brick wall the rest of my life. One of the nuns there said all marriages were not made in heaven and blessed by God, but at this point, I was still determined to try.

My then-husband Larry had again been in and out of treatment centers and was seemingly doing okay. He was also taking a drug called antibuse to deter him from drinking—or so I thought he was taking it. Money was an issue for us since he would lose a lot of time at work from either drinking or being in a treatment center. I tried to work in the evenings so he could watch the children. One night, when I was at work, I got a phone call from the kids. They were at my neighbor's house, the ones we went to the Al-Anon meetings with. They told me that their dad was drunk and acting crazy. I left work and came home, the children came back from the neighbors with me, and for the first time, he became violent and tried to strike them. He was angry because they called me and let me know he was drunk. I, right then and there, made him leave, and although I cared about him, I loved my children more. I knew he would never be back in my home again. I knew then I would divorce him, and even the pope himself could not have talked me out of it.

I was not making much money working in the group home and could really not count on much help at that time from the alcoholic. I went to our government for assistance, and literally they told me to sell my house and car and use that money and then come back. They did give me food stamps for approximately two months. I talked to an attorney who advised me to sell my home and pay off all bills, even though some of the bills were in my ex-husband's name only. The attorney said they could still come after me for payment. The first couple of months were tough financially, but miraculously, the money would appear when I needed it for bills. Like a reimbursement for something I forgot about that wound up being $150—the exact amount I needed to pay a bill. Christmas came a couple months later. All the teachers at my children's school where I volunteered showered the children and me with gifts of toys, clothes, and food. We also received valuable emotional support from my family members.

Also during this time, my friend Laura (who encouraged me to get into real estate) said she knew a salesperson looking to share his subdivision, I took the job. I sold a house the very first week, and it was a spec house (a completed home). I earned $5,000 for the commission. I knew that getting the real estate license was not a waste of time and money but was ultimately a blessing from God that saved my children and me from poverty.

I was teaching catechism at that time, and I was nervous about selling the house and renting an apartment. A friend who cleaned homes explained to me that I could make good money cleaning homes part-time and still work around my real estate job. My friends at St. Mathias put an advertisement in our church paper and also had it placed in two other church papers for no cost. I quickly had nine homes to clean every other week, which would more than cover my rent. My brother Joe and his wife Judy even had me start cleaning their home and paid me quite generously.

I sold my home, but there was a problem. We sold it FHA, and a condition of the sale was replacement of the roof, which would cost thousands that we did not have. God took care of this, as my nephew Skip that did home improvements agreed to do it for only $500. The best part is he agreed to be paid after I closed on the home and had money. Then, of course, the week before I was moving, the dishwasher broke. The builder I went to work for quickly got me one at his cost, which was more than affordable. God does provide when we have a need.

We moved into an apartment in the area so the children could stay in the same school and church. The divorce was final, and I got full custody of the children. I received child support when my ex-husband was working, but it was always months behind schedule. He ultimately still owed me thousands of dollars after they turned eighteen, when he declared bankruptcy. He never did have to pay the remaining money. I was never angry about this because God provided me with more than enough money to care for myself and my children. I felt truly blessed. I truly felt bad that Larry could not bring himself out of his addiction to alcohol, which later wound up taking his life at only fifty-one years old. He loved his children and was a good person who had been taken over by addiction. May God bless his soul.

I continued to go to church and decided before I would date, I would like a church annulment. That way, if I did meet someone, I would be free to marry in the Catholic Church. The process that some call invasive was actually quite healing. It takes you back through childhood and pre-marriage relationships. I found out because of my father's alcoholism, I felt the most comfortable in a relationship with someone who was on the road to and eventually became an alcoholic. Therefore, I did not enter into that marriage an emotionally healthy person. The best part of the process was that they would grant me the annulment only if I would continue with the Al-Anon, which I may not have after the alcoholic was divorced from my life. This would help ensure that I was healthier and would not repeat the same unhealthy marriage choice.

I had sole custody of the children but did allow them to see their father when he seemed to be stable. On one particular occasion, that judgment proved to be wrong.

Stacy was around ten and Brad, eleven. They were out with their father and his new girlfriend. I get a phone call from Stacy saying she was at some party, and they were all doing drugs. While she was speaking, the girlfriend grabbed the phone from her and yelled at her and told me everything was fine and hung up. I called my old neighbor Vicki: the angel of a friend that lead me to Al-Anon and the kids to Alatot and then Alateen. We were not sure what to do or how to find them, so we prayed.

Minutes later, the phone rang. It was my little girl Stacy. She and her brother were safe at a stranger's home. After the phone call, she pretended she was playing outside with her brother and some other children when she talked her brother into going to a home in that neighborhood and asked to use the phone. For a child of this age, I thought it was brilliant, and it was a blessing she chose the house of a good man.

The man got on the phone and gave me directions. My friend and I picked them up promptly. Their father and his girlfriend did not notice them missing for hours, but when they did, they came to my apartment and screamed at me from outside. It was truly an answered prayer for Stacy to have the intelligence to help herself, and Brad to trust in her to go along. Thank you, Lord, again for this and the many other times you protected them from harm.

The next year, I had great financial success and was even able to cut down the house cleaning business to five homes instead of nine. My best friend Beth and I planned to drive to Disney World in her minivan, taking our children the day after Christmas.

I was getting a little nervous about going since my homes were closing, and I didn't have a lot of new deals. Then, as usual, the deals came when I needed them. We drove down to Florida and camped at a KOA near Disney World, and we all had a great time. We decided to go to the space center and got a flat tire on the way. Unfortunately, the highway we were on had very few exits and was surrounded by the everglades.

We were standing outside of the van with the children wondering what to do. Not too many people had cell phones back then, and we didn't either. A greyhound tour bus driver pulled his bus over and told us to quickly get the kids inside the van because alligators were prevalent in that area. We did just that, and then he called the closest service station for us from his cell phone and told us to wait in the van until someone came.

This man, who had a tour bus of people, took the time to warn and help us. This was surely from God. The tow truck driver said he could not fix it there, so he towed the van and fit all six of us somehow in his truck. The repair was not expensive and we were on our way. Looking back, I can see how we were truly blessed by that tour bus driver stopping. We do not know what we would have done had this not happened.

Losing Mom and Meeting Mike

In January and February of 1992, Mom was going in and out of the emergency room with breathing issues. While she was in St. Joseph's in February, the doctors finally diagnosed the problem as a kidney blockage. She was otherwise still healthy, living on her own, driving, cooking, and going to church. The only solution they offered us was to do an angioplasty to remove the partial blockage of plaque in the renal arteries. Mom was not afraid, as she had the same procedure years earlier on another heart blockage, and it was very successful.

They moved Mom to St. John's hospital in Detroit to do the procedure. It was only supposed to last a half hour, but two and a half hours later, they were still trying to clear the blockage. That night, Mom told my sister and me to take off her slippers. We told her that she did not have any on. That was the beginning of what they called a "snow shower" of the plaque particles. The doctors told us she may lose a couple toes, and that she would be fine. But both of her kidneys were damaged by all the plaque particles, and she would need dialysis. The nurse in dialysis said, "I shouldn't be telling you this, but I have seen this before and she will probably lose both of her legs and ultimately die." Unfortunately, that is exactly what happened.

After I received the news, I went to my church chapel at St. Mathias. At that time, the chapel was open twenty-four hours. I had a talk with God. I prayed, I was sad and worried, and told God, "I thought we had decided I would have at least one year without another death." As if I knew what His plan was. I prayed, "Please at least send me somebody to love and help me through this." The very next day, I saw an ad in the newspaper for a "parent without partner" dance and felt I should go. So I called my friend Beth from the Port Huron area and asked her if she would like to go with me. I explained to Beth that I would want to stay with my mom until visiting hours were over, so it would not be until later. Beth explained it would work perfectly with her plans, as she would be in the area and going to a movie with her sister. She planned to meet me right after. You can truly tell when it is God's design, because things just seem to fall into place.

I walked into the hall and was immediately asked to dance. As I looked around the room, I locked eyes with a tall and hand-some gentleman who made his way toward me and also asked me to dance. I agreed, forgetting I had already told the other gentleman I would dance with him. The other gentleman ended up walking away, unhappy with my choice.

My dance partner Michael and I talked, laughed, and of course, danced. We went out for coffee afterward with Beth and another gentleman. As Beth and I were leaving, Michael asked me to go out the next night to a concert. I said, "Wow, that is fast! Usually you talk on the phone first." His answer to me was, "I have a feeling if I don't ask you out now, that I may be sorry the rest of my life."(I later found out he had broken a date with someone else to take me to that concert.)

The next couple weeks after the concert, we talked constantly. Even though I was working, or at the hospital, I squeezed in time in for him.

While Michael and I continued to get to know each other, my mother's condition was getting worse.

Unfortunately, the nurse's prediction proved to be true. They amputated both of mom's legs and then she died a couple of weeks later. God did bless her. She was a special lady with a lot of faith, and she died on Good Friday that year. We buried her on Easter Monday.

I had only known Mike for three weeks at this point, but he was there at the funeral home and met my entire family—even ones that were from out of town. I later found out what a sacrifice that was for him, since he never went to funeral homes. I met his family and four children on Easter Sunday, while taking a short break from the funeral home (which just happened to be across the street from his home). He courted me and also my children, as he would bring us gifts and take us shopping along with his own daughter, or even to basketball games. He gave me a ring (no, not an engagement ring yet) after only six weeks. He said he did not want other guys to think I was available.

After about a year, he asked me to marry him. We went through the programs at the Catholic Church, planning to get married there and also built our home at the same time. I had already had an annulment, so I was able to marry in the Catholic Church. However, I found out a couple of months before that Mike, who was not even Catholic, would need an annulment from his first wife because they were married in a Lutheran Church.

Because of this, we got married at a civil ceremony, and I did not attend communion, which saddened me deeply. Mike, who had been attending church with me before, was no longer going. Although, he knew it was important to me and proceeded to go through the annulment process he started before we got married. The pastor at the church noticed I would be teary-eyed during the communion and would not receive the Eucharist. I explained the situation, and he took over Mike's annulment process and said he would marry us there as soon as it was finalized. He also said that if I, in my heart, felt this is a good Christian relationship, then I should attend communion because God does not want me to feel separated from him.

Following this, Mike would attend church periodically. He finally made the decision to become Catholic and attended the RCIA program. He was baptized that Easter, and when his annulment was completed, he was able to receive communion at our wedding. If we have faith and patience, God does have a way of helping things come out right in the end. God is good.

LIFE IS FRAGILE HANDLE IT WITH PRAYER

Craziness on the Employment Front

My marriage was great, work was successful, and my daughter Stacy had gone from being my hostess and aide to being my partner. I trained Stacy and the builder's daughter. He had a subdivision for us that was being delayed (it wound up taking several years) so he had no place for us to work. The painter who worked for him was also a builder, though I did not particularly care for him. He came to Stacy and I and offered us a job, which we were hesitant to take. After we saw his model, however, we knew it was a good layout to sell. He needed us to set everything up, including employees, for the Builder's Association Home-A-Rama. The Home-A-Rama went well and we sold quite a few homes. At first, he was quite a good builder and was honest with us.

Then things started to change. This builder had financial problems, as he was building a mansion for himself and he already owed a lot of money before we even started working for him. We started having to insist he put in the items listed on the contracts. He began to question what was in the contracts, even though it was very clear as to what was included in them. We built and closed all but the last three homes when things got very bad. People were calling on homes we closed telling us there were liens or, even worse, contractors trying to get money from them. He put in maple cabinets and tried to convince the buyers and myself they were cherry cabinets that the client's had paid for. I called the cabinet shop and verified my work order said cherry, and the cabinet maker said the builder told them to build them with maple instead.

The last straw was when we found out he had never put the deposit down on the lots he told us he had bought in the next phase and lost them to another builder. This was our chance to confront him and leave. We only had two homes left in construction, and they were close to being complete. We had finished all work orders and let the clients know we would still complete their sale but would no longer be in the model. We had already spoke to the builder we were originally working for and he offered us a job. At the same time, a larger building company had called to offer us a job as well.

Both of those opportunities, along with any others, faded as the builder and his brother blacklisted us and tried to spread lies that we took money from him. Stacy, my brother Ed and myself confronted the brother and even asked them to bring in a police detective if they felt we had taken a penny. We told him we would be happy to cooperate, and they assured me they would stop bad-mouthing us and they would pay us. They did neither. We wound up getting a lawyer and suing him, only to get a portion of the money he owed us.

Needless to say, we put in applications everywhere, and after almost four months, we were offered two jobs. Our trust in builders was low at this point, so I said to Stacy and my friend Donna, "I guess to know which builder is the right one, I expect God to send Jesus down on a cloud to show us." I again said this to Stacy just before we went in for our third interview with a builder. We had been to the office before, but had never been out of the conference room. As they gave us a tour of the office, there stood an eight-foot statue of Jesus on a cloud. Stacy and I just looked at each other and never said a word, but knew this was the job we would take. God has a real sense of humor and knows my skeptical heart. He knew a small statue on a desk would go unnoticed or be written off as a coincidence. God is good.

The Story of Wendy

Wendy was a friend through our husbands, Jim and Mike, who also golfed together. We really did not see each other very often but had fun together when we did. We even took up golf at the same time, taking lessons together. In addition, we also went to plays and dinner as couples on several occasions. Wendy was only fifty when she passed away (just a couple years older than myself). We really never know what kind of impression we leave with people, but when she found Jesus, she immediately sent me a card and wanted to share that with me! I was so happy for her we called and chatted, and I could not have been more delighted.

I was sad to hear about a year later that she was diagnosed with lung cancer and had only six months to live. She decided to undergo chemotherapy at the insistence of her husband, stepdad, and sister. I decided I wanted to visit Wendy and pray with her and asked my friend Donna if she would like to come. Donna, who is a friend from church, had said yes initially. The next day, Donna called me and said she had a dream and she felt I was supposed to ask Mary Ellyn, a friend of mine through my brother Ed and sister-in-law Mabel who also had a cottage near mine. We really did not know each other very well at the time. Donna had met Mary Ellyn when I invited her to come along with Donna and me to a class at Sacred Heart Seminary. I promptly called Mary Ellyn and told her the situation with Wendy and asked her if she would go with me to pray. Mary Ellyn was quiet and then tearful. She said, "I just prayed last night that God would use me again in this way."

My next hurdle was to call Wendy a new Christian, but a non-Catholic, and see if she was open to the idea. I was happy when she responded, "Yes, I would love that." I think when you are doing God's will, that things can literally fall into place.

We got together at first every couple weeks, and then weekly. Mary Ellyn had some experience at this and said we must pray the two of us before and after we pray with Wendy to ensure that we are protected from the devil or anything else that might come against us.

Mary Ellyn would often pray in tongues, which Wendy thought was beautiful. Wendy told us that when we prayed with her she felt the peace of Christ rest upon her and had a break from her pain. Mary Ellyn often asked God to give her a dancing heart and Wendy knew and felt exactly what that meant.

She was worried about one of her Catholic friend's falling away from the church and asked us if she could invite her to come the next time we prayed, and of, course we encouraged it. We even got this friend to get more involved at church so that she would feel closer fellowships.

We learned many things about Wendy; she never had any children of her own but sort of adopted her single girlfriend's children, and she and Jim would help them out financially on a regular basis. They did this with many other friends and relatives when circumstances warranted.

At this point, Wendy knew the chemotherapy would not work and was okay. She was now on a mission to help everyone in her life discover Jesus in the personal way she had before as she put it, "It was too late." You could see it in her eyes as she tried to help them understand this.

Mary Ellyn and I were there with her family and friends at her home, they had moved the hospital bed into her great room. She was in extreme pain, struggling to breathe, and when she saw my tears, she reached up her arm to hug and comfort me. I remarked that I should be comforting her, but she just smiled and said, "It is okay." She had no fear because she was secure in her faith.

Wendy was part of my deepening of faith, and for that, I am thankful to her for letting us minister to her.

The Story of
Rosemary's Passing

I n July of 2008, my mother-in-law was found to have a spot on her bladder that was later diagnosed as cancer. They tried to put a stent in her kidney a couple of weeks later, only to find out it was covered with cancer. This is the story of her final week on earth.

Mike and I were up at our cottage along with Kathy, John, their children, and their friends Connie, Mike, and their children for the Labor Day weekend. As you can imagine, with six children ages seven and under, it was quite chaotic but lots of fun. We were cleaned up and ready to leave to return home early Monday morning when we received a phone call from Joe (Mike's stepfather and Rosemary's husband of forty years). He had said they were taking her to the emergency room. We kept in contact on the drive home, so we would know if we should reroute and head toward Monroe instead of home, as it is nearly one and a half hours away from our home in Macomb Township. Joe assured us we did not need to come, as she had not even been admitted. No sooner did we get home from our two-and-a-half-hour drive from the cottage when Joe called again informing us they were admitting her to intensive care and also that she had suffered a heart attack.

We have never spent a great deal of time with this part of the family because of the distance and other various factors. I feel God used this as an opportunity for us to be closer to them. Mike had even suspected his only sister, Jeannie, was perhaps mad at him since she was often home and never came over to say hello when Mike visited his mom and Joe over the previous years. Jeannie's home is a mother-in-law suite that is attached to Joe and Rosemary's home. We did not see anyone the first day but Eric, who is Jeannie's daughter's son. Mike commented it almost seemed like they did not trust us and did not want us alone with his mom. The next day, we saw Jeannie and she greeted Mike with a big hug and seemed to be happy he was there.

We were only home that week for one night and a couple hours and mainly stayed at a hotel near the hospital. Whenever Rosemary was in the hospital or rehab prior, I would always ask her if she minded if I would say a prayer with her and she always agreed. Now the background is that part of the family never attended church. In fact, praying seemed foreign to them. I learned that Rosemary had been Catholic, and when she divorced and remarried, she, as many others, thought she was excommunicated. I again asked her if she wanted me to pray with and for her. She said yes; soon, one of the hospital nuns came in. I asked the sister if she knew my friend Fr. John Britto, since he used to be the hospital chaplain there. Fr. John is the same priest that did the anointing of the sick for my brother Larry. The sister did know Fr. John and was delighted to talk about him and even gave me messages to send to him. She also led some prayers with Mike, Rosemary, and me, and when she was finished, she asked Rosemary if she wanted to receive communion and she did. (I consider this to be a reunion with Jesus.) We were told Rosemary did not have long and that she would decline rapidly, which she did. After praying with her one day, she said to me, "It's okay. I am tired and I have been talking with my mom." I was amazed at the fact that someone who did not have a lot of faith in her life could jump to having no fear and being so sure of her faith just like that. As those of us who have faith know, God is merciful and loving and he has the same reward for someone who had a lifetime of good works and faith as a person who accepts Jesus at the last hour. Her acceptance made it a lot easier for Mike to accept what lay ahead. He would literally sit there holding her hand for hours, sometimes talking to her and sometimes silent. All of Mike's children got there that week to visit, essentially saying good-bye. The last couple days, they moved her into a room to die. They had coffee and cookies for us, and I got a second recliner so both Jeannie and Shelley could have one to spend the night there. Rosemary was surrounded by loved ones literally 24-7. We all got closer with her and with each other. Shelley and Jeannie left on Saturday morning when Mike and I arrived, and her husband Joe was there as well. Rosemary's breathing started to get shallower, and while Mike was holding her hand, she took her last breath. He quickly took his thumb and made the sign of the cross and said, "I claim you for Jesus Christ." I am not sure what inspired him to do that, but my guess is it was the Holy Spirit.

As we meet with the funeral director to talk, I learned Rosemary wanted to be cremated and did not wish to have a viewing. The director suggested a priest, and again since religion was so foreign to them, they said no. I was thinking we cannot just have her ashes there and not do anything to give her a Christian send-off, so I spoke up and said I would, with the help of Kathy, my daughter, do a prayer service. I had no idea of how to do it but felt God was leading me to do this and it would all fall into place. The good news is, since they were cremating her first, we had almost a week to prepare. It did fall all into place. First, Kathy agreed to find and read two Bible readings. Secondly, I prayed and wrote a little program, which contained song, petitions, the readings, and the Lord's Prayer. This was quick and easy to write. (It always is when you are being guided by the Holy Spirit.) Then, I prayed again and wrote a eulogy, thinking it would be difficult. But again, when God wants you to do something, it comes easier than you would imagine. It seems all the stories and happenings of the previous week had helped me to get to know Rosemary in a different way, and also write the eulogy in a manner that conveyed her in a warm and loving way.

One thing uncompleted was the music; of course, God had already picked it for us. How you ask? Mary Ellyn, who is one of our prayer warrior friends and very in tune with God speaking to her, shared that as she continued to pray for Rosemary and Mike the week she was dying, she keep getting the song in her head, "I Have Loved You." She was not sure if the message was for Mike or his mother, but God assured her it was for both. This made sense since I know Mike's fear was that his mother was not a Christian and worried what would happen. The words are so true in that song: "I have loved you with an everlasting love, I have called you and you are mine." I called my church to see if they had it at any Catholic stores, and they did not. I looked up the author online to find it was contained on a CD entitled, "On Eagles Wings" and was at a bookstore near Mike's office.

We put some pictures together with other family members, I ordered flowers from ourselves and our children, added a background and Rosemary's picture to the service booklet, had it printed, and then we were ready.

We arrived early and went straight to Joe and Rosemary's house in Dundee and then to the funeral home. I arranged the flowers, putting the one from Mike and me, which was a moss and floral cross, right next to the podium where Kathy and I would speak. The funeral director took the CD and said he would play both songs on cue, one at the beginning and one at the end. I had printed the words, and they were included in the service booklet I had made. My brothers and sister and spouses all arrived along with some of our close friends, and all our children and grandchildren. Moral support was there. Kathy's in-laws from Cincinnati, Ohio, had even arrived to help John watch the kids while Kathy and I did the service. I asked them to pray for me during the service along with our good friend Mary Ellyn as well.

The music began and people sang along. I got very flushed, but the words flowed and everything went beautifully. People responded when they were supposed to, and everyone said or read the Lord's Prayer. (I printed that in the program just to be sure all who wanted to could participate.) Many thanked Kathy and me, some wanted to know what church we were ministers at. (I think that meant we did a good job.) I spoke briefly with Shelly that day, and the girl who was not comfortable even saying the Our Father had bought herself a necklace with a prayer box charm and said she would pray.

Amen. God is good. Even with things we may perceive as bad, good can come from them. God can take any situation and bring light and goodness.

The Story of Judy

Judy was my sister-in-law and my friend. We spent lots of time together, traveled often on fishing and gambling trips. We were always just plain comfortable with each other. Judy was an only child, so I think that intensified our closeness. She had her grand-daughter, who is mentally challenged, living with her, so Haley and Judy would come up to my cottage for a few days with me before the rest of the gang got there. We had such great times.

Judy was a Jewish girl who went to a Catholic boarding school, St. Mary's of Monroe. She would often attend church functions such as weddings and funerals. A few years before her death, she started to wear a cross around her neck. I quickly joked and said if she ever got sick, that I could baptize her. She smiled and said, "Okay!"

Judy was having some health issues when she was at the cottage for the second year in a row, so I insisted she get to the doctor. I also told her that I would hassle her until she did. Unfortunately, they found a mass over her ovaries and omentum. It was cancer, and at that time, they said it was ovarian cancer. They scheduled the surgery to remove the cancer on Labor Day weekend. I went to my priests at St. Isidore and asked if in this special type of circumstance we could baptize Judy without her going through the year-long classes. Her chemotherapy would weaken her and she would not be up to the task.

They agreed. When I offered this option to Judy, she was thrilled. We were able to baptize her before the surgery.

A year went by and the chemotherapy caused neuropathy, leaving her with difficulty walking. We had been bugging her to get a second opinion, so she went to U of M for testing and found out it was not ovarian cancer, but rather gastrointestinal cancer. She also got a third test to verify this.

Then, in October of 2010, she decided to let U of M treat her and went back. It was the day of my niece Jennifer's memorial, and she insisted her husband (my brother Joe) go to the memorial to represent them. All four of their children went with Judy to U of M. There, they got the shock of their lives when they were told how bad the cancer had grown, and she had only three to four months to live. They did not recommend chemotherapy, as it would only add six weeks to her life and would not add to her quality of life. The Karmanos Cancer Institute disagreed and tried to get her to undergo more chemotherapy. Judy was about to start the chemotherapy when, as I like to think of it, "God intervened." The Karmanos nurse called to let Joe know that their daughter Shannon had requested too many records, and she would need to go through the records department to get them. Joe said to the nurse, "I saw your face when Dr. Choi was talking about the chemotherapy, what is your opinion?"

She said, "I really cannot talk about this."

Joe pressed on and said, "Off the record, what do you think?"

She said, "Honestly, if it were my loved one, I would not put them through the chemo."

Joe said thank-you and then said a small prayer: "Dear God, please help me. How can I dash her last hope?" At the same time he walked through the bedroom door, Judy was hanging up the phone and heard the entire conversation. An answer to Joe's prayer, she had heard the entire conversation and she said that she didn't want the chemotherapy.

During the following months, she had good and bad days but quickly accepted her pending death and helped us all prepare. She picked out all the readings and songs, and even the people to do them.

I could not sleep for several nights and was arguing with God: "I am not ready to write Judy's eulogy." Yet the thoughts kept flooding my mind until one night I said, "God, you win." And I got up and wrote the entire thing. It was less than two weeks later when Judy asked me if I had written it yet, because she wanted to hear it. Yes, of course; this is why God needed me to get it written so we could share it with Judy herself. I read it to her and she said it was perfect, but that I failed to mention her three grandchildren. (Okay, God, so Judy caught my mistake; again, you do know better, Father).

Judy said to me, "You know, I have to have a new outfit wherever I go." I knew she was unable to go, so I volunteered. She explained that she wanted a blue outfit. I went to the store, and all the winter dress items were on clearance and an additional 50 percent off. Plus, after telling my circumstance to the clerk, they came up with another 20 percent off coupon. The blue ones were just simply not something I could see Judy in. I spotted a champagne snake-style print with a beaded black color and beaded buttons and a black skirt. It was beautiful. A $298 outfit for only $50, and best of all, it looked like something Judy would wear. I was nervous about showing it to her because it was not blue. It was at their house a couple of weeks later when Joe said, "Let's show it to Judy." Joe loved it. The first thing Judy said was, "It's not blue."

I quickly said, "The blue ones were ugly, and this is a $300 outfit that is classy, like you. And I could picture you buying this."

She motioned for me to bring it closer and she felt it and said, "Quality." She loved it!

Judy was worried about being buried in the Catholic Church, since she had been ill and never formally joined a church. I called and asked my pastor, Fr. Mike, if we could have her funeral at St. Isidore, where we had her baptized. He called me back and left a beautiful message that I was not to worry about this; of course, they would have the funeral there.

Judy was relieved when I told her and had some songs she wanted to use. So I then got a booklet for funeral planning from the church. We went over, and she picked all the songs and readings except one Joe wanted: "Amazing Grace." Judy even picked the people to participate, including six of her nephews as pallbearers. All this was done by end of November.

Christmas came, and by then, Judy was pretty weak and mainly in bed. But she rallied for her children and grandchildren for their family's Christmas Eve celebration. On Christmas, Judy and Joe would have Mike and me over for breakfast and then go to the casino. Her son Erik volunteered to cook breakfast this year, and we would wait and see how Judy felt about going to the casino. I had my doubts, thinking she would be exhausted from the day before. We walked into the house, and she was dressed and ready to go. She even ate a little breakfast and had a mimosa. That day was truly a gift from God, and a wonderful memory. She was as funny, witty, and charming as always. She was in a comfort chair, so I stayed close by to move her around and take her to the restroom if she needed. I feel so blessed to have been able to get more quality time with her.

As Judy got weaker, I spent more time with her. I even started to spend one or two nights a week and slept right in the room with her to tend to all her needs. One day, when I was there and she started losing control of her bowels, Joe and I were cleaning her up, only to have to do it again half an hour later. Judy kept apologizing, saying, "I am so sorry."

I just said, "Hey, you know how you always say can I do anything for you when someone you love is sick? This is SOMETHING."

She promptly replied, "I would do it for you."

I answered her, "I know you would." Then we had a nice cry together. She never apologized to me after that because she understood it was actually a gift for me to be able to help her in this way.

I would always bring communion for Judy and Joe when I visited, and we prayed together. One day she said, "I wonder what heaven is like, no one knows." I answered her that this is not true. I told her about Akiane, a child prodigy born to atheist parents who draws and paints pictures from things revealed to her by Jesus. She has painted and described heaven through her poetry as well. I was able to bring up on my droid phone the Youtube CNN interview with Glenn Beck, which was Akiane at age sixteen describing her paintings, poetry, and visits with Jesus. She also described heaven having colors so beautiful that we could never imagine. I also was able to show Judy an interview with a little boy named Colton Burpo, who at age four, was in a coma for five days and when he came home started describing all the dead relatives in detail. He saw his mom feeding his baby sister and told her that he had met his other sister. The mother was shocked as she never shared that she had a miscarriage. It was determined that Colton had been to heaven. He described Jesus and heaven in the exact way that Akiane Kramarik did. In fact, in his book *Heaven is for Real*, it was explained that the little one was brought many pictures of Jesus and he would find something wrong with all of them. One day they brought up Akiane's painting of Jesus on the computer and waited and then said, "What is wrong with this one?"

Colton replied, "Nothing, that's him."

Gianna Jessen, a saline abortion survivor, was another video I showed to Judy that day on Youtube. Gianna has a testimonial about how she survived because God wanted her to share her story, which she does worldwide. Judy said that it was such an inspirational visit. I felt blessed that I already had this knowledge and could share it with Judy when she needed it. God is good. He prepared me well. I also told her it was okay to be afraid and that I would be too. We are afraid even when we are starting a new job. She smiled and agreed. It was some time after this when Judy described to both her daughter Shannon and myself that the colors are so beautiful.

On Monday night, the family called and had hospice put in a pain IV that went directly into Judy's port. She was no longer in any pain, but also was not really able to communicate much either. I went over on February 9 to help Joe and spend the night. The first thing I noticed that morning was that when we changed her brief, it had a strong ammonia odor. I cleaned her and covered her with ointment to protect her skin.

The nurse came in the morning and said we were on the final leg of the journey. I asked if I should skip my Wednesday night commitment to Welcome Home Catholics, and she said it could be days yet or even a week. Something must have changed her mind because before she left, she said it would probably be a good idea if I stayed both nights. My sister Anita came that day with John, and she continuously helped me change Judy, cover her with ointment, moisten her mouth, and talk to her. The two little nuns that she volunteered with at St. John's Hospital came to visit that day and said upon leaving that they would pray for her to go quickly. Anita and John left, and Anita said the same thing. Joe and I both called it a night at around 8:00 PM. I was on an air mattress on the floor next to her bed when at around 9:00 PM. I could hear a change in her breathing. I got up and sat next to her and could hear it. It was the same Cheyne-Stokes breathing that was described in the booklet. I pulled the cover back and her legs looked like marble, as described as mottling. I knew then I had to wake Joe up, as it was getting close.

Joe and I decided to call Shannon, and she suggested putting the oxygen mask on her and also the finger monitor so we could see how fast her heart was beating and how low the oxygen level was. Joe then called the other three children. All of us were with Judy, talking to her and we prayed the Our Father with all our hands on her, and her breathing stopped. She was gone. Joe kept saying it could not have been more perfect with everyone there together. The next day we met with the funeral home, and I met with the deacon at St. Isidore, and I was a little tired, but I made it to my Welcome Home Catholic session and felt comforted by those who I was welcoming back. (Funny how that works.)

The funeral was beautiful, and I was comfortable reading the eulogy and everyone seemed to think the entire mass, including the eulogy, was great. I have included it next.

Judy's Eulogy: Oy Vey

"Oy Vey," as Judy would often say. This is not an easy day for us. Reflecting upon Judy, these are things that came to mind.

Judy was known by many names and wore many hats. She was fondly referred to by my Dad as Judy the Yahoody, which referred to her Jewish heritage. She was called Gambleina by her co-workers for her love of gambling and frequent trips to the casino. Mike, Joe, and I nicknamed her the Dessert Nazi because on one of our trips to Las Vegas, upon ordering desserts, she quickly interrupted us, telling the waitress what each of the four of us wanted. The three of us sat there dumbfounded while she ordered for us. This quickly became a joke, and Judy would tease us that if we did not behave she would not allow us to order dessert. Judy earned yet another nickname when we were on one of our many golfing, fishing, and gambling trips to the Leelanau Peninsula. We were on the second or third hole of the golf course when Judy insisted her foot hurt and played with one shoe the rest of the eighteen holes. We quickly dubbed her with an Indian name, "Judy One Shoe." She was always a good sport and even embraced these titles, joining in on the fun. Her formal name Judith she tried to get to catch on but only a few of us used it, and not that often.

Judy wore many hats: loving wife, mother of four, grandmother of three, sister-in-law to ten, aunt to twenty-one nieces and nephews, great-aunt to nineteen, and even great-great-aunt to two. Not bad for an only child who often said she married my brother Joe for his family.

Judy was many things to many people; to my mom she was an answer to a prayer for her son Joe, who was often the cause of her worries. Mom was so happy that after a short while, she did not mind that her Catholic son was marring a Jewish girl with two children. She quickly fell in love with Judy, Shannon, and Jeff. Mom loved them as her very own. As I recall, the word step *was NEVER used by anyone in the family. Make no mistake, we all fell in love with Judy, Shannon, and Jeff. This*

45

past December, trying to show support to her son, my nephew Jeff I said, "Do not worry, we will get through this together." He quickly responded, "But she is our anchor."

Joe, Jeff, Shannon, Danielle, and Erik: Do not worry, she still will always be your anchor, through the things she taught you, the way she lived her life, and even the way she embraced her death.

Judy was a fountain of good advice that you could count on. A great friend and not the kind that agrees with you all the time. She always told you the truth and was not afraid to. Judy built strong relationships and knew they could weather a disagreement or redirection. I believe all her relationships with her children, grandchildren, husband, relatives, and friends were solid, for to know Judy was to love her. I personally looked at her as a big sister when I was young, sharing her clothes, babysitting for her, etc. I could always count on her for good advice, although sometimes unsolicited. One particular time in my life when I was a single mom struggling financially, I had put an ad in my church paper to start a house cleaning business just to make ends meet. I told Judy about this and she and Joe immediately insisted on me cleaning their home; a few years later, they did the same thing with their next-door neighbor, letting her clean their home when she was struggling financially. Judy had a heart of gold and was always offering a helping hand.

Judy was a Jewish girl but went to a Catholic boarding school, St. Mary's of Monroe. She knew a lot about the Catholic religion. Judy would always go to church for family anniversary masses, funerals, and weddings. I think she always believed, but many years ago, not sure exactly when, Judy started to wear a crucifix around her neck. I was quick to tell her that if she ever got sick I could baptize her myself, she smiled and agreed. Little did we know years later, her being baptized would be a reality. When Judy was diagnosed with cancer, I went to my church and explained the circumstances and they agreed to baptize Judy here at St. Isidore. When I knew this was a possibility, I presented the option to Judy and she quickly responded yes. I am her godmother. Judy's faith was always growing over the years. In fact, I cannot tell you how many times people who met her and knew my brother Joe would state matter of factly, that Judy must be some kind of saint to be married to Joe. To know Joe is to love him too, they had a special bond that was tested over forty-two years of marriage, but only strengthened. The love they showed each other even at the end was something to witness. The loving caretaker he was to her and the way she always comforted him through her final days.

Judy amazed me that when she found out that they had treated her for the wrong cancer and she had three to four months to live, she was not angry; she was not sad. Judy knew she had done the work; she had strengthened her relationship with God and accepted Jesus as her savoir and had complete trust in Him. Although I am sure there was sorrow to leave us, she hid it well and said she would accept God's will for her. I think this came easily to her because she knew it is not "Good-bye," but simply, "See you later."

The Story of Ed

My brother Ed was a good friend to me, and an advisor especially on my career; he was my golf buddy and my friend. He and his wife Mabel introduced Mike and me to our good friends Tony and Mary Ellyn Merpi who bought a cottage at the same time we did near Ed and Mabel. The six of us took many golfing trips together, Hilton Head, Williamsburg, Myrtle Beach, and Florida.

I was saddened to find out Ed had pancreatic cancer, and it did not look good. He did chemo for a little while but choose to live out the rest of his life with no chemo. He no longer had the cottage as he had sold it to our sister Anita, but over a two-year period, I planned many get-togethers with the family and friends at the cottages. We went golfing, gambling, wine tasting, boating, played table games, and just spent lots of quality time together. Ed told us he did not want us to be sad but strong, so we were. He had a great relationship with God and strong faith. He never complained, although he had to be in pain, he was accepting and even uplifting to those around him. There was a change in him, though; he never missed an opportunity to give a hug or say "I love you" even to the men in his life.

Mabel, thinking it was a bad thing was forced to take a buy out and retire from AT&T or lose her pension, little did she know God was clearing her schedule to be there for Ed, as he was diagnosed with in a short time of this. As I told you before, sometimes we think something is bad, and it turns out God was giving us something we needed.

The last time I golfed with him and Mabel was about two weeks before he died. It was a Sadie Hawkins Tournament, and he would not be my partner because he was not golfing well do to his illness. He was concerned about my score; he thought I had a chance of winning. Mike and I golfed as a team but played with Ed and Mabel, thanking God for this last gift to us!

Ed went home and decided to go into the hospice program. He called each one of us siblings and told us he had begun the hospice program.

I was able to stay with him when Mabel went to a shower and had a wonderful day with him, also had dog duty as Christopher their youngest son was out of town and they were dog sitting.

Chris got back into town and spent some time with his dad; again, thank you, God, for this gift. On September 11, 2013, Tom, their middle son, called and asked me if I could stay with his dad at around five o'clock so that his mom could take him to get his car. I said sure. I received a text from Mabel just before I arrived, telling me to let myself in, so I did. I went up to the bedroom, and Ed was in a chair in the bathroom with his head down, Mabel at his side. She had accompanied him to the bathroom since he had just started on a drug that made him wobbly. Mabel said after he went to the bathroom, he got up and was very unsteady; she told him to told hold onto the sink and ran and got a chair out of the bedroom as Mabel said the angels must have held him up because he immediately sat and his head dropped down and eyes closed. I called Mike my husband upon seeing this, and I thought it might be the Cheyne-Stokes end of life breathing but not sure we decided Mabel should call the hospice nurse. Meanwhile, she called Jason her oldest who came immediately, Tom got home, and Chris happened to be close by taking his dog to the vet and was right there too. The hospice nurse confirmed he was near the end. Mike and Ed and Mabel's sons moved him into the bed with the permission of the nurse to make him more comfortable. The nurse said it could be a couple minutes or a couple hours. Elizabeth, the youngest and only daughter, was all the way across town doing her first parent-teacher conference and there was a severe thunderstorm. The boys kept calling and asking if she was almost done, taking care not to tell her too much so that she did not have to make the long drive in the storm upset. Other family members arrived, Mabel's siblings, my younger brother, and his wife. We all prayed with him, led in prayer by Mabel. Elizabeth arrived more than a couple hours later, and Ed was still alive; he was waiting for her, I am sure. God is good! She came in and held his hand; I think she even got in the bed. Ed somehow acknowledged her and was at peace and then passed away with all of us there. God was there, making sure Mabel was not alone, making sure his children were there. Ed did not want to have to wear diapers; he did not need too. He did not want to have heavy pain killers; he did not take them. He wanted us to be strong for each other and we were. Ed was such a good Christian role model that I think is why God blessed him with many extra quality months of life beyond what they predicted. He was also blest with really living life to the fullest right until the end.

Avielle's Birth

Stacy, my baby girl, was having her first baby; she called early in the morning and Mike and I met her and Sean at the hospital on December 20, 2014. Things were progressing along, Sean's parents had arrived too, and the baby was even in the birth canal; contractions were regular and getting closer. Suddenly, the baby left the birth canal and labor seemed to stop, so in an effort to move things along, they put Stacy on drug to speed up the contractions.

Sean's mom and I were talking to a nice young lady wheeling her baby down the hall. Her name was Somme. She had just had her fourth baby. I asked her nationality, and she said she was from Iran; she proudly stated, "I used to be a Muslim, but I am a Christian now."

Sean came down the hall to take a short break, and Somme was giving birthing tips to him to take back to Stacy. I asked Sean if he minded if I go check on Stacy; he said, "Good idea." I opened the door, and to my horror, Stacy was surrounded by many staff members. I asked, "Is everything okay?"

And they shouted, "NO! Emergency C-section."

I said, "Should I get her husband?"

They said, "Absolutely, get him quick."

I ran down the hall and shouted to Sean; he ran back to the room to get ready for the operating room. I was crying and visibly shaken, and Somme saw this and quickly said, "Would you like me to pray with you?"

I said yes. Sean's mom, Debbie, Somme, and I held hands; and Somme prayed the prayers I was too distraught to pray. I walked back into the waiting room and the little white-haired volunteer said to Sean's parents, Dennis and Debbie, Mike, and myself, "I see your daughter is having an emergency C-section. would you like me to pray with you."

We said yes. I felt God was giving me a sign things would be okay. We soon heard the lullaby on the speaker system, signaling a birth; we hoped it was our baby. Sean sent the nurse to let us know it was, and Mommy and baby were fine. Somme also heard this and came in to ask us if they were okay. I let her know they were. I asked Somme what made her think to pray with us. I told her I often do that with strangers in distress but had never been the recipient. She said she went back to her room after praying with us and asked herself the same question as she had never did this before. I told her I knew why, God wanted to reassure me and used her, and I thanked her for listening to God's request.

God is good!

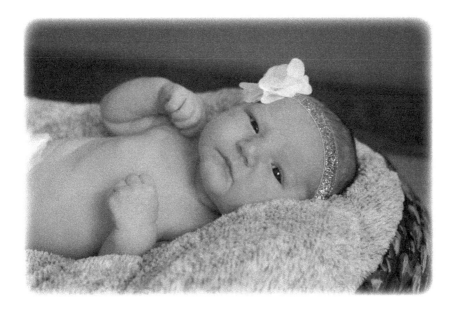

My Friend Edie

Sometime in 2001, I was asked by my church to visit and bring communion to Bud Bockensette as he was on hospice for colon cancer! It was then I met his wife Edie at that time still in her eighties. I would speak with Bud alone first and then visit, pray, and give communion to Edie and Bud! Little did I know this was the start of a beautiful friendship. Bud passed away in September of 2003; I asked Edie if she wanted me to continue visiting, and she was delighted. We would share everything in our lives births, deaths, sicknesses, etc. I watched as she turned ninety and showed off her many birthday cards to me. I was there when she had to suddenly move out of her condo. Edie's condo was very close to my home and church. Her family was moving her into a senior center over a twenty-minute drive away. Edie was so sad when she was telling me about the sudden move as she was sure I would no longer visit her! She was so excited when I assured her that was not the case, and I intended to continue to visit her.

Edie was in and out of the hospital, and I met all her children over the years. I believe it was good three or more years before Edie passed after the doctors said because of the hardening of her arteries around her heart that she would probably not make it out of the hospital and if she did would be in a nursing home. *Wrong!* We at this time over several visits planned and picked all the music and readings for her funeral mass. She would often worry there was not enough room for all those in heaven. We talked about heaven often she asked if she would recognize people, and I told her that many people who have had near death experiences say they were greeted by loved ones who have passed. It was then I asked Edie if she would be one of my heavenly greeters; she smiled and agreed. I often reminded her of this, and I look forward to it and seeing her again and getting one of her wonderful hugs! We prayed always together about health problems of loved ones and special intentions. One of the things we would pray about was her grandson Patrick who did not know he belonged to her son or her family. We often talked about before she died writing a letter to let Patrick know that although he did not know her, she always loved and prayed for him. Patrick's mother had left the state and married someone else, not telling Patrick the truth. It was just a few years ago when, through Facebook, they contacted him. Patrick was in the military and lived in Hawaii with his wife and four children. It was a beautiful thing that upon learning of this family he never knew, he flew all the way to Michigan with his wife to meet the family he never knew, and of course, Edie too! Edie was ecstatic and showed me many pictures of the reunion. He later came for another visit, and he and his wife brought their four wonderful children and Patrick's mother in-law and father-in-law even came to meet the Bockensette family too. This I believe was an import thing to Edie and was on her unofficial bucket list. God is good! Edie lived on her own at Jefferson Meadows in her own apartment for the next three years. She loved to knit and made and gave hats to everyone as a sign of love. She made them for Mike and me and our grandkids too. She always made enough for her entire family for Christmas, and it was a tradition they all enjoyed. I believe it was a year before she died that one of her grandchildren did a photo album and even had a large collage made of everyone wearing Edie's hats. Even grandson Patrick from Hawaii with wife and kids were in the pictures wearing their knitted caps in Hawaii! She was so proud to show me the album and collage! Edie even gave me a copy of the collage! What a wonderful thoughtful thing to do while she was still around to enjoy it!

Edie celebrated her hundredth birthday on July 29, 2015 with a party given by her children. She was like a queen receiving her subjects. She was very pleased to meet my husband Mike in person after years of stories and seeing many of my family pictures. There were many of her friends from the past that came along with her many grandchildren from out of state and some from out of the country! It was clear she impacted many with her joyful personality! I feel blessed that I was one of them!

Three Babies

I know you probably guessed by now that I am a ducks-in-a-row kind of gal, and with childbirth, you just have to go with the flow and give it to God!

The end of September was the due date for our daughter-in-law Zuzana. Zuzana's mom and brother were in from Slovakia. On her due date, we went to Brad and Zuzie's for a visit with her family.

Mike had a once-in-a-lifetime business trip to Louisville, Kentucky, hosted by one of the other trustees. We were even invited to attend races at Churchill Downs (home of the Kentucky Derby) seated in a suite in the millionaire row. I was prepared not to go as it was so close around the due date. Zuzana's mom was still here from Slovakia; her younger brother had to fly back home and miss the birth. Baby Mathew was overdue. Minutes before Mike was leaving, driving with our friends, Zuzie called me. Her doctor had scheduled her to be induced on Monday after we would be back from our long weekend trip to Louisville. Zuzana felt she would not go into labor until then. She and Brad really did not want me to stay home and miss the trip. I had, at this time, found out I could use our bonus miles and fly back home if the baby did come before Monday. Off I went, and we had a great time. Many memories were made. God is good!

Zuzie was to be induced on October 3, and our daughter-in-law Meg had a scheduled C-section on October 11. We had a great time and arrived back home about 3:00 p.m. on October 1.

October 1 brought us the first of three new grandchildren. She was three weeks early and was delivered via C-section. Her name is Meara. We had literally just gotten back into town an hour prior from a business/pleasure trip to Louisville! We were there for Meara's early arrival when needed. God is good! Prayers were answered. Both our daughter-in-law Meg and baby were healthy! Meara arrived October 1, 2016, at 5:15 p.m., six pounds, six ounces, nineteen inches long!

Two days later, our daughter-in-law Zuzana went into the same hospital to be induced. Her mother was in from Slovakia. We had Sammy there with us just a week shy from turning two. We spent most of the day, Grampy and I, keeping Sammy entertained. Zuzie's mom does not speak any English, so she could be limited in helping and, at one point, almost went into a diabetic shock. It looked like a long night, so my husband, a.k.a. Grampy, went home. Our daughter Kathy threw some of things in a suitcase and brought them to me.

I insisted she come in to check on Zuz as she was in severe pain, and the nurse would not call the doctor to check her. Kathy took over comforting Zuzie with cool washclothes and told Brad to insist they check her again. Sure enough, they then wanted her to not push until they could get a doctor to the room. Fifteen minutes later, Mathew was born, another healthy grandchild. God is good and praying works!

We brought Sammy back into the room; he was less than thrilled to see the baby. This was apparent when they handed Zuzie the baby to be wheeled out to her room from the birthing room. Sammy, at the sight of this, had a heartfelt sob that literally brought me to tears for him too! Brad and Zuzie saw this, and after they settled Zuz and baby Mathew into bed, she made a spot on the other side, and Sammy climbed in! It was a great move on their part! Sammy now, when anyone visits, immediately takes your hand, pulls you to Mathew, then holds his hand out and says, "Ta-da!" Adorable!

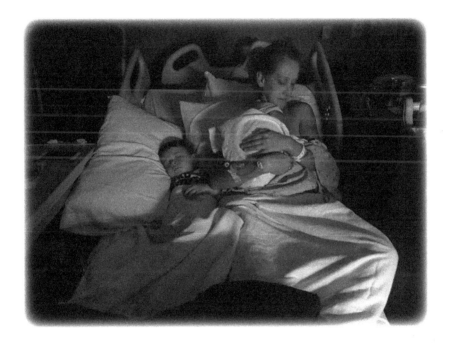

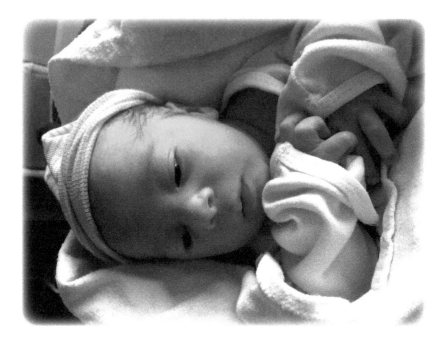

Mathew Bradford, born October 3, 2016,
9:28 p.m. (7 lbs 7oz., 20 inches long)

Everything was going great. We were planning a trip to visit Philadelphia in October, and since the first two babies were already born, we knew we could make it. Life was good. We would have a nice visit from October 13 to the 17! We had our normal basketball games with the grandkids. We had an award ceremony for our fifteen-year-old granddaughter. We were very proud she ranked in the top 100 students for grade point average in Metro Detroit.

We are always praying for our children and grandchildren. It was when I met Bette my daughter Kathy's mother in law, that I added their future spouses as well. This is something Bette did for her two sons starting when they were just children, maybe even babies. So she was praying for Kathy since she was a little girl! It is great to have co-grandparents that are such strong Christians. They have become my prayer partners through life. Thank you Ken and Bette. I have also learned over the years when you are too distraught to pray, you can simply say the name Jesus and that is a prayer itself. I can tell you first hand this always works. It will quickly calm me enough to keep praying in an emergency. Mike and I pray together for our children, grandchildren, family and friends as needed. We always pray together before we start to travel for God's protection and can not tell you how many times those prayers have saved us. God is good.

We had our planned visit to Philadelphia to visit our daughter and family in October. We had a wonderful visit with Stacy, her husband and daughter. We went to a children's museum, a festival in the park, dinners out, and even the pool!

In November we were blessed to have the three of them come from Philly for a visit. We enjoyed our time knowing that she would be too far along to come for Christmas and we would not see them until January or so we thought.

It was December. We were thankful we had Stacy and Sean in from Philadelphia with Avielle for Thanksgiving. Looking at her then, I thought no way she would make it to her scheduled C-section just two days before her January 6 due date.

Okay, let's get to the birth of baby number 3. On December 20 at 5:00 a.m., I received a call from Stacy. She said, "Poor Avielle. She not only has her birthday five days before Christmas, she now has to share it with her brother. My water broke." Then Stacy told me Sean and Avielle both had the flu. They were trying to get someone to come to the hospital; they had very few choices. I said I would try and find a flight, and Grampy would drive the eleven-hour drive. We literally had to cancel Christmas with our other children and grand-children. You go where needed as a parent, and since they are all parents themselves, they understood. My husband would drop me at the airport and continue on. It was on the eighty-minute drive to the airport that I realized I booked the one-way flight from Philadelphia to Detroit. A phone call and $200 later, it was corrected.

I was at the airport and worried about stowing my two car-ry-ons because they had announced limited space and that they may have to check some of them. I was standing and talking with a nice gentleman from Philadelphia when they had announced this. I told him about the emergency C-section. He said that he was seated in first class and to come with him so I could be in the first group to board. He told them I was with him, and they seated me in the first group. I am thankful to God that this man was quick-thinking and kind. This meant I did not have any checked luggage, which saved me a good half an hour of time.

I texted Sean just before takeoff, and he sent a pic. The baby was born. Both mom and baby were healthy. God is good. I could be on the flight without worrying what was going on. I landed, found the taxi area, and arrived at the hospital within twenty minutes. I had gotten a text from Stacy with her room number.

I was happy to be there and see them. They had held off the C-section until Sean could get someone there to watch Avielle. One of the moms of Avielle's playmates came but could not stay long. She was relieved by Summer, their babysitter, who is also a nursing student.

Once the baby was born, they let Avielle see mom and baby. Cameron Ryan was born six pounds, five ounces, nineteen and three-quarters inches long, at 10:38 a.m.

They then told Sean they could not come back until they were twenty-four hours symptom-free. Summer followed Sean and Avielle back to their apartment and watched after Avielle until she had to leave at 6:00 p.m. My husband arrived from Detroit at 6:30 p.m. The next morning, Sean went to urgent care, where they gave him two bags of IV fluid. They told him he was dehydrated and that he had a superflu. This flu was a combination of several flus. He felt much better but far from healthy when he returned home that morning.

Stacy and I spent a decent night at the hospital. She had a spinal block for her C-section, and they poked her four times, causing excruciating pain down her leg before they got it right. She was not only recovering from the C-section surgery, but she had to deal with that same shooting pain and temporary nerve damage. We kept the baby in the room. I slept in what I refer to as a scissor chair. It would lean back and feet come up, but if you moved forward at all, it would spring back to the sitting position.

This area of the hospital had been neglected as right after the New Year, it was being torn out for remodeling and moving maternity to a new wing. That explained the lack of attention to the room. I found a dried french fry on the bathroom floor. There was a water leak and puddles on the bathroom floor, and the room heating system was dirty, blowing cold air.

The next day, Stacy was better. We had a wonderful nurse both nights, who was very helpful and attentive. The next day, they took the catheter out, and Stacy got out of bed and even took a shower with my help. Baby Cameron had his circumcision, and we asked to go home. Sean and Avielle were doing better but still sick. Sean picked us up and had us home by 3:00 p.m. on December 22. Grampy had stayed home with Avielle.

Sean had sterilized everything and had plenty of Clorox wipes. We agreed that no one but Stacy or me would hold the baby until they were twenty-four hours symptom-free. That night, Mike got sick too. I sent out a Facebook post asking for prayers. God protected Stacy, myself, and baby Cameron; none of us ever got this horrible superflu. I discovered Instacart and was able to have coconut water, fruits, veggies, cereal, bread, and even a pot roast for a Christmas dinner all delivered to our door. Grampy was literally in bed for two days. Stacy was unable to sleep in her bed anyway due to the soreness from the C-section. We both slept on the large L-shaped sofa with a recliner on each end. Baby Cameron slept in a raised bouncy seat right next to us. Cameron was just what we needed: a great baby who slept a lot and was never really that hard to care for. He later got acid reflux and colic, so this calm and peaceful baby was truly a gift from God.

Four days later, on December 24, Sean could finally hold his baby. He made sure Avielle did not feel left out.

On Christmas morning, Grampy was feeling better. We gave them their privacy so they could let Avielle enjoy her Santa gifts and they could bond as a family. I had gotten up early, put the pot roast in the slow cooker, and made some coffee. We had shipped Avielle's presents, so we got to enjoy her unwrapping them. Grampy felt much better and was able to hold Cameron for the first time.

The pot roast turned out great. We were all healthy at the same time. This was the best present ever. We talked to our other children, wishing them a Merry Christmas and planning to celebrate on New Year's Day. Sean was well enough, gradually taking over my duties of helping Stacy recover and watching Cameron. We left on December 28, knowing they were in good hands. We had a major prayer answered, which I had been praying often for, and that was that Stacy and Sean would move back to Michigan. They would arrive back in Michigan to live in March. This was an unexpected joy.

The Journey Continues

I am still on the journey and will continue to add the highlights of my faith journey to share with my children and grandchildren. I found God everywhere in my life and feel so blessed to have the unconditional love and guidance of God our Father, Jesus, and the strength from the Holy Spirit.

Praying, to me, is sometimes formal as in the Our Father, but mainly talking to God directly and trying to listen for the answers. Believe me, God will keep trying to get a message to you until you listen. This can be through Jesus speaking in the scriptures, through another person, or just a feeling that comes over you, like "Aha! I understand now, Lord!" I feel I have been given many signs from God over the last few months that I am to publish my faith stories; if you are reading this, I was right! God is good!

I pray my family will all have a strong faith that becomes their compass through life. I know with a strong faith they can get through anything life may throw at them. May God bless you and yours.

CPSIA information can be obtained
at www.ICGtesting.com
Printed in the USA
BVHW021827101119
563403BV00006B/12/P